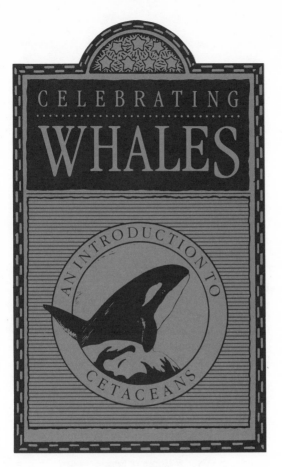

CELEBRATING

WHALES

AN INTRODUCTION TO

CETACEANS

by Nick Beilenson

Illustrated by
Martha Holland Bartsch

PETER PAUPER PRESS, INC.
WHITE PLAINS · NEW YORK

Assistance in providing materials and answering
questions is gratefully acknowledged to representatives
of The American Cetacean Society (whose Whale Fact
Pack and *Whalewatcher* journal were particularly
useful), Animal Protection Institute of America, Animal
Welfare Institute, Center for Marine Conservation,
Cetacean Society International, Greenpeace, The
Humane Society of the United States, International
Wildlife Coalition, Long Term Research Institute, Sea
Shepherd Conservation Society, and The Whale Center.
The staff of U.S. Congressman Anthony C. Beilenson
and of the Subcommittee on Fisheries and Wildlife
Conservation of the House of Representatives were also
of assistance.

Special thanks is due to Dr. Robbins Barstow,
volunteer executive director of Cetacean Society
International, for his critical review of the text.

Errors and omissions are of course the responsibility
of the author.

N.B.

Table of Contents

Introduction

And God created great whales.

GENESIS 1:21 (KJV)

Whales are just incredible! These mammals, which together with dolphins and porpoises comprise the order of cetaceans, are a delight and a mystery, right here on earth.

They are big. Some in fact are immense. The largest of the whales, the blue whale, can be 100 feet in length and weigh 150 tons. In contrast, an African elephant weighs 6-7 tons and a hippopotamus 4 tons. Even the largest of the dinosaurs probably weighed only 85 tons. Of course, the whales have a crucial advantage: the buoyancy of the ocean supports their weight and they have no need of massive legs to support their body mass.

They are smart. The sperm whale has the largest brain ever to appear in an inhabitant of this earth. The humpback whale not only sings songs but creates new ones over the course of time. Dolphins and porpoises have exhibited intelligence in the wild, and have been taught to perform intricate tasks. Some scientists believe that in the future we will be able to "interview" them using a form of language.

They are mysterious. No one knows how, or often why, they emit the incredible sounds that they do. What do they do with those large brains? How do they communicate and find each other in the vast oceans?

They are gentle with, curious about, and sometimes friendly with humans. An occasional behemoth, who would view us in size as we would view a mouse, will gently glide by a scuba diver without touching him. "Friendly" gray whales allow themselves to be touched and petted. Friendly dolphins are an occasional but worldwide phenomenon.

They symbolize . . . something. Many types of whales are endangered. Since whales are at the top of a complicated oceanic food chain that starts with microscopic plant and animal organisms, saving the great whales may necessitate safeguarding their entire watery environment. They are thus a conservation symbol. To some, whales may represent a mystical or spiritual power in nature. To others, the interplay of humans and cetaceans may underscore the need to truly share the planet with all its living creatures.

Cetaceans

Whales, porpoises, and dolphins comprise the order of cetaceans. Generally speaking, the larger ones are termed "whales" and the smaller ones "dolphins" and "porpoises."

Cetaceans are warm-blooded mammals, maintaining a constant 87-degree body temperature. Although creatures of the oceans, they breathe air and cannot survive underwater without frequent surfacings to renew the air supply in their lungs. They feed on vegetation, fish, and other sea creatures (krill, squid). They have complex social behavior and stay in touch. Their brains are large. They court, males compete for females, and they mate. The females deliver live young, who then nurse for about a year, and retain bonds with their mothers. They get sunburned. They play. Many relate to us in a peaceful and gentle manner, even though we have slaughtered them for centuries.

Sound familiar? Yes, whales and other cetaceans are a lot like us. They are certainly much more like human beings than they are like fish. They were lords of the sea for millions of years; it is only in the last few centuries that mankind has usurped their domain. Let's take a closer look.

Whaling History

*Death to Moby Dick! God hunt us all, if we
do not hunt Moby Dick to his death!*

HERMAN MELVILLE

The killing of whales may have started with
the Norsemen and Arctic natives 3,500-4,000
years ago. In the 900's the Basques of Spain
and France began to harpoon the right
whale, and the English and Dutch followed
in the 1600's hunting the Arctic right whale.
In the New World, Native Americans hunted
whales from their canoes before the arrival of
the Europeans. In the 1760's New Englanders
began extensive hunting of the right whales,
using the whalebone for corsets, bustles,
buggy whips, and other flexible items, and in
the early 1800's started seeking the sperm
whale worldwide for its special oil, used for
smokeless candles and lamps.

Nineteenth century whaling voyages lasted
2-4 years and might result in a catch of only a
few dozen whales. When a whale was sighted
and the lookout cried "Thar she blows!" a
25-foot whaleboat with a crew of six would
be lowered and give chase, either under sail
or by rowing. When the boat was but a few
feet from the whale, the harpooner would

propel his 8-foot harpooon deep into the whale. If the whale remained on the surface, rather than dive, the whalers would be taken on a "Nantucket sleigh ride." When the whale at last tired, its lungs would be pierced and it would bleed to death. The crew of the main vessel would then strip the whale of its blubber, remove the baleen plates or whalebone, and draw off its oil. Whaling was hard, dangerous work, and sometimes fatal for man as well as whale.

In the period 1830-60, the United States dominated the whaling industry, its whalers operating from Boston, Nantucket and New Bedford in Massachusetts; New London, Connecticut; Sag Harbor on Long Island, New York; and from San Francisco. Thereafter, American whaling went into a steep decline; many whaling vessels were sunk during the Civil War, and domestic, inexpensive kerosene rendered whale oil uneconomical.

In this century, most whaling has been carried on by Japan, the Soviet Union, Norway, Iceland, and other nations. The traditional "cold" harpoon has been replaced by the explosive grenade harpoon that kills on contact. Sailing ships have given way to steamships capable of outrunning any whale. Factory ships accompany catcher boats, and can remove the valuable parts of a whale in an hour. The difficult, "romantic" whale hunt of the last century has been replaced by a technologically advanced slaughter.

Before tracing the save-the-whale movement of the past two decades, let us explore how whales function and note the distinctive characteristics of the major species of whales.

Toothed v. Baleen Whales

Cetaceans appear to be descendants of mammals that lived on the land. They are closely related to artiodactyls such as hippopotamuses, camels and cows. The oldest group of whales, the ancient whales or Archaeoceti, appeared about 45 million years ago, but died out about 25 million years later.

Scientists have identified at least 76 different species of cetaceans alive today. They are divided into two major groups: Odontoceti or toothed whales and the Mysticeti or baleen whales.

Toothed whales include the giant sperm whales, beaked and bottlenose whales, belugas, and narwhals. Toothed whales have a single blowhole, an external nostril on the top of their heads. They have teeth in their lower jaws only; generally, these teeth are utilized to grasp fish, squid, and other prey, which are then swallowed whole. (Dolphins and porpoises of the family Delphinidae are loosely identified as toothed whales but have identical conical teeth in both the upper and lower jaws.)

Toothed whales are known for their ability through echolocation (akin to sonar) to navigate and to locate their prey. They can determine how far away and in what direction an object is, and what its external and possibly even its internal (i.e., bony) configuration is.

The contrast with baleen whales could not be sharper. Baleens include most of the "great" whales, including the blue, fin, sei, Bryde's, minke and humpback of the rorquals, the right and bowhead (right whales), and the gray whale. They have two blowholes rather than one.

Baleens are the "strainers" of the sea. Instead of teeth, they have rows of long baleen slats or plates that hang from the

13

roofs of their mouths, with a hairy fringe on the inner edges. Baleen (sometimes called "whalebone") is made of a fingernail-like substance. In order to feed, baleen whales merely take in enormous quantities of seawater and then force it back out through the baleen. Quantities of small prey and krill (animal plankton) are trapped and swallowed. Feeding may be done through "lunging" (the rorquals), "skimming" (right whales), or "grubbing" on the ocean floor (gray whale). Rorquals even have pleated grooves on their undersides which allow their throats to expand to take in several tons of water.

The baleens are believed to navigate and communicate through the emission of sounds. Humpback males in the same location "sing" a common song. And bowhead whales, also baleens, use acoustic communication (calls and countercalls) to hold a group together, and are able to identify and avoid ice floes at a distance of 500-1,000 yards.

The Senses

Hearing is clearly the key sense used by cetaceans. Small cetaceans (porpoises in captivity) have been found to respond to tones of between 150 and 153,000 cycles per second (the human range is from 350-20,000 cycles per second). Significantly, tones in the range above human ability to hear, the supersonic range, penetrate longer distances in the water than lower tones. And in fact, sounds in general travel much farther in water than in air—and about four times faster.

The echolocation practiced by toothed whales and the songs of humpbacks are of course based on the whales' sense of hearing.

Whales can see quite well, and will often take a look at a boat or other above-water object by "skyhopping." But the range of vision is severely limited even in shallow water, and some whales dive to depths that are pitch black.

Whales do appear to have a sense of touch. They are seen rubbing up against one another or touching during mating or play. The knobs on the heads of humpback whales are thought to enhance their sense of touch. Friendly whales and dolphins seem to respond to petting and touching by humans.

The sense of smell appears to be absent in whales. The sense of taste appears to play no role; whales swallow their prey whole.

Breathing

A whale is a spouting fish with a horizontal tail. There you have him.

MELVILLE

As mammals, whales must breathe to live. Every few minutes, they come to the surface, and expel a mixture or stale air and water vapor up through their blowhole or blowholes. This mist is clearly visible, and since the "blow" of each type of whale is unique either in height, size, number (one or two), or angle, identification of whale species can often be made from the "blow" alone. The sperm whale, for example, emits a single cloud of mist up to 24 feet high in a diagonally forward direction. Strong muscles seal the blowholes while the whale is not blowing, and a splash deflector also protects the blowholes.

Sperm whales dive for over an hour, blue whales for up to 50 minutes, and fin whales can stay under the water (without breathing) for 15 minutes. Whales seem to be able to fill their lungs almost completely, to store excess oxygen efficiently in their blood and muscle tissue, and to tolerate a lack of oxygen for a limited period.

The breathing of cetaceans, unlike that of

their terrestrial cousins, is not automatic and involuntary. They must consciously come to the surface and exhale and inhale. This means that whales are never fully "asleep," but rather assume a resting state (where a group sometimes breathes in unison).

Flukes, Fins, and Flippers

The flukes of cetaceans are their horizontally oriented tail fins. (Fish have vertical tails). They usually have a central cleft. The flukes of the bowhead whale can measure 25 feet from tip to tip. Fluke muscles are so powerful that whales can propel themselves through the water at up to 20-30 knots.

Most cetaceans have dorsal (back) fins of varying lengths, although Arctic species such as the bowhead and beluga have no dorsal fin to interfere with swimming under floating ice. Most impressive (and sinister) is the tall, triangular dorsal fin of the killer whale.

Flippers, which are front limbs, also vary greatly in size, the humpback having especially long flippers (up to about 16 feet). Some cetaceans can rotate their flippers in a semi-circle, and use them for balancing, braking and steering in the water, and for caressing during courtship.

Cetacean Acrobatics

Porpoising occurs when a whale, dolphin, or porpoise leaps out of and back into the water with a graceful, arching movement. Breathing occurs during this movement.

Breaching is the movement of some whales in which they thrust themselves upward out of the water with a tremendous thrashing of their tails. Often their entire body will be exposed in an almost vertical position.

Lobtailing happens when cetaceans raise their flukes out of the water and then smack them on the surface. This resounding slap can be heard for miles, both above and under water.

Flippering occurs when whales splash the water with their flippers. Often a number will join in the fun.

Tailsailing is seen when, on a windy day, whales lift up their flukes at right angles to the wind and allow the wind to propel them along. Researcher Roger Payne has seen right whales ride the wind, then return to the starting point and exuberantly repeat the exercise over and over.

Spyhopping whales extend their heads vertically above water into a position where they can take a look around.

Mating, Calving, and Rearing

Cetaceans engage in courtship (flipper caressing, rolling around, etc.) and mating at various times of the year, not just when the female is in heat. Thus, mating may have a bonding as well as a reproductive function. In some species, one male may assert dominance, while in others females may mate with multiple partners. It is theorized that a "sperm competition" occurs: males with large testes can deliver more sperm, which crowds out the sperm of their rivals.

Mating takes place sometimes while the two whales are floating on their sides (gray whales), or with the male underneath the female, belly-to-belly (right whales). The males have long flexible penises tapered at the end (sort of like thick rubber hoses) which, considering the size of the participants, their smooth skins and lack of "handholds," and the motion of the water, are absolutely essential equipment. Sometimes a "helper" or "auntie" (who is probably a male) stays alongside to steady the female.

Females bear calves every 2-3 years, after a gestation period that ranges from 8-10 months for a harbor porpoise to16 months for a sperm whale. Calves are generally born tail first (presumably so that they need not

19

breathe before being brought to the surface immediately after they are fully free of the mother), but gray whale females have been known to deliver their calves on the surface, head-first.

Calves nurse from 6-24 months. Mother's milk is incredibly rich; the milk of the humpback, for example, has a 45-50% fat content. The mother will protect her calf from enemies, keeping it close to her in its early weeks, and will play with the calf. This bond sometimes continues after weaning.

Predators

With the exception of man—and that is an all-important exception—the only predator of whales is the killer whale. Killers hunt in packs and can wound or even kill the gigantic blue whale. They will also seek out the calves of right whales, sperm whales or other species. One researcher, Tom Arnbom, reported seeing 20-25 killer whales attack about 30 sperm whales off the Galapagos Islands. The sperm whales "drew their wagons in a circle" around the lone calf in the group and, apparently using their jaws and flukes, were in that instance able to fend off the pack of killer whales.

Types of Whales

1. Humpback Whale

He is the most gamesome and light-hearted of all the whales, making more gay foam and white water generally than any other of them.

MELVILLE

Humpbacks, together with blue whales, fins, seis, Bryde's, and minkes, are "rorqual" whales. These are baleen whales which have on the underside of their bodies long, pleated throat grooves (down to the navel) that expand when the whales feed, allowing them to engulf enormous quantities of food-rich water for filtering through their baleen.

Humpbacks (so called because they arch their backs as they dive) have round bodies, mostly black in color, and run 40-50 feet in length and 25-40 tons (including up to a half ton of barnacles).

Humpbacks have unusually long, white, knobby flippers, and their flukes (tail) have serrated trailing edges. They also have head bumps (called "stovebolts" by early whalers) which actually contain hair follicles and may give the humpbacks a certain sense of "touch." The black-and-white patterns on the undersides of the flukes (which can be clearly seen when the humpback dives) and other coloration variations permit the identification of individual humpbacks.(This enables groups like the International Wildlife Coalition to have Whale Adoption Projects.)

A humpback whale, either alone or in a group, sometimes feeds by expelling a stream of bubbles under its prey to form a "bubble net" or "bubble cloud." It starts the "net" 50 feet down and gradually forms a cylinder of bubbles up to the surface, compressing the prey into a small area. Finally, the whale, open-mouthed, lunges upward through the prey, sometimes breaching in spectacular fashion.

Humpbacks are remarkably acrobatic whales, and may do backflips when they breach. They sing beautiful songs, and burble, rumble, and snore when asleep (resting). Population estimate: 10-12,000.

Marine Mozarts: Songs of the Humpback Whale

Humpback whales sing long, complicated "songs," consisting of a regular sequence of repeated sounds (whistles, clicks, groans, squeals, and unearthly moans), that last up to half an hour. All the whales in an area will sing the same song at any given time, but not in unison. While the humpbacks are in their Hawaii or Bermuda breeding grounds, the local song (different in the Atlantic and Pacific) will gradually change, but will remain unchanged while the whales summer in the Arctic. After five years, the song will have changed so greatly as to be unrecognizable.

Roger Payne, who helped popularize this phenomenon and who has studied it for many years, concludes that the humpbacks create or compose as they go along, behavior otherwise seen only in humans. In addition, since the humpbacks in one locale all sing the same song, the leader (or leaders) is clearly able to communicate the changes to the others. All whale songs follow the same rules of composition, and long songs appear to include patterns equivalent to rhyming in human speech. So far, no one has heard a humpback returning to one of the old songs.

All singing humpbacks are males. Thus, it is suspected that the songs are part of a male dominance ritual, like the display of antlers by land mammals.

The *how* is as unknown as the *why*.

Humpbacks have been seen underwater singing their song (detected through hydrophones and strong underwater vibrations) without expelling a single bubble of air! But one singer was spotted moving his flippers in rhythm with his song.

The songs of the humpback have been "translated into human music" onto the record "Whales Alive." Paul Winter and Paul Halley transposed, and Leonard Nimoy narrated.

Voyager Space Probes; Star Trek IV

While we don't know what if anything humpback whales are conveying or "saying" through their songs, humankind is not taking any chances. When the United States in 1977 launched the spacecraft Voyagers 1 and 2 towards other possible sentient beings in our galaxy, recordings of classical and rock music were included, as were greetings in 55 languages and a communication—message if any unknown—from a humpback whale. Perhaps he has already received a reply!

Whale contact with extraterrestrials is also pivotal to the plot of *Star Trek IV: The*

Return, a motion picture released in 1987. An approaching alien space probe wreaks havoc upon the earth. Dr. Spock deciphers noises emanating from the probe and realizes that it wishes to communicate with a humpback whale. But this is the 23rd Century and humpbacks have been exterminated! Not to worry. The crew of the spaceship *Enterprise* returns to present-day Earth, transports some humpbacks into the future for some humpback-alien space probe palaver, and Earth is saved. The moral: humans and the other creatures of the earth are interdependent; we will survive or disappear together.

2. Sperm Whale

No creature that has ever roamed the land or inhabited the seas has had a brain as large as that of the sperm whale. What it can do with that brain, other than make powerful clicking and other sounds (presumably to locate, and perhaps stun, its prey) is simply unknown.

The sperm whale is the largest of the Odontoceti or toothed whales. Its massive head is one-third the length of its body (unlike any other whale) and contains a huge Spermaceti organ in its forehead, site of the sperm oil so precious to 19th Century whale hunters. In fact, no sperm or reproductive fluid is contained in this organ; it is theorized that the organ is actually used to magnify sounds made by the sperm whale.

Male sperm whales grow to about 60 feet in length and weigh over 40 tons; females are much smaller (not the case with baleen whales), attaining 40 feet in length and weighing only 14 tons. One-ton calves are born after a 16-month gestation period. Interestingly, in summer these whales separate into "bachelor pods" which migrate northward, while the females and calves remain in the tropics.

Sperm whales have a light-brown to blue grey color, not at all like that "great white whale" of fiction, Moby Dick, and their bodies have a rippled appearance. Sperm whales have a single blowhole on the left side of the head. Their powerful flukes can reach 16 feet in width.

Sperm whales have enormous teeth in their lower jaws that fit into sockets in the upper jaw. These teeth are probably used to grasp, but not chew, the giant squid that furnish the bulk of the sperm whale's diet, until the squid can be swallowed whole. (Because the sperm whale can swallow large organisms whole, it is clearly the most likely whale to have swallowed Jonah.) To reach their prey, sperm whales dive to depths of 3,000-5,000 feet, perhaps deeper, staying underwater for more than an hour!

The sperm whale has been designated Connecticut's state animal. The current worldwide population of sperm whales is estimated at close to 1 million animals.

3. Blue Whale

Blue whales are the largest creatures on earth today, averaging about 75-80 feet in length and 110 tons in weight. (One taken in 1909 measured 110 feet.) They emit the loudest sounds of any living being. The calves of the blue whale, born after a year's gestation, weigh 4-7 tons, as much as a mature bull African elephant! Each day the calves gain 200 pounds, as they nurse on 100 fat-rich gallons of mother's milk.

A blue whale consumes 3 million calories a day, every day, and may live a full century! They eat mainly small, shrimplike krill. They can dive at least 350 feet, and stay down for an average of 10-20 minutes at a time.

The bodies of these smooth whales are blue-gray on top, with mottled white spots over most of the body. Their 20-40 inch baleen plates are black. Underneath they are whitish in color. However, in cold waters, diatoms, yellowish micro-organisms, attach themselves to the undersides of blue whales, and for this reason blues are also called "sulphurbottoms."

Blue whales have long, thin flippers, a tiny dorsal fin, and relatively small flukes. They can be identified by the chevron-shaped patterns on the back of their heads. When diving, they show their entire flukes above water, unlike other rorquals.

Blue whales can be found in all the oceans, but only perhaps 10-15,000 of this endangered whale survive.

4. Fin Whale

Second only in size to the blue whale, the fin or "finback" whale (named for its prominent falcate or curved dorsal fin) is long, sleek, streamlined, and extremely fast. Its nickname "greyhound of the sea" is well earned. It is a rorqual.

Mature fins average 65 feet and may reach a length of over 85 feet and a weight of 80 tons. They have a single ridge on the top of the head, and a chevron-shaped light patch behind the blowholes. Fins are dark gray to brown on their top and sides. Unique to cetaceans, they exhibit asymmetrical coloring. Dark coloration extends lower on the left than on the right. The right lower jaw and front third of the baleen on the right are white, yellow-white or pale gray, while the entire left jaw and baleen are dark.

The blow of the fin whale is shaped like an inverted cone and is 20 feet high. Fins take 15 minute dives to a depth of at least 750 feet. They feed mainly on small crustaceans, sometimes balling their prey into a tight circle by swimming around them, before enveloping them in a single gulp. They turn on their right sides before gulping; it is thus surmised that their asymmetrical jaw pattern provides a camouflage effect.

Fin whales have been individually identified in New England waters by plotting subtle differences in the jaw-baleen pigmentation, varying patterns of the chevron mark, the profile of the dorsal fin, and notches and body scars.

Fin whales are quite social, often traveling in large groups. Their estimated worldwide population of 100-125,000 occurs in all oceans, but mainly in the Southern Hemisphere.

5. Sei Whale

This baleen whale is the fastest of all the rorqual whales, attaining speeds of about 25-30 knots. Seis run 50-60 feet in length, and weigh about 25 tons. They are streamlined, have one long ridge from the tip of the upper jaw to the blowholes, and have a tall falcate dorsal fin. Seis have a galvanized appearance, are dark gray above with white on the chin, throat and belly.

Seis feed by skimming near the surface with a partly open mouth (as the right whale feeds) for huge swarms of tiny crustaceans. They have 320-380 baleen plates on each side of the upper jaw. Seis dive for 5-10 minutes at a time. Calves are born after an 11-month gestation period.

Their name (pronounced "say") comes from the Norwegian "seje" or pollock (similar to the cod), since the seis appear off Norway each year at the same time as the pollock. Seis follow their food fish, and are found in all oceans. Population estimate: 50,000.

6. Bryde's Whale

Bryde's whales inhabit the tropical and subtropical oceans. Though smaller, they are very similar in appearance to sei whales, but can be distinguished by the three prominent ridges on their rostrums or tops of heads (the sei whale has only one ridge). Bryde's whales have 250-350 baleen plates on each side of the upper jaw.

Bryde's feed in the more normal up-and-down rorqual pattern, rather than skimming for food; their dives are from 5-15 minutes. Their diet includes schools of mackerel and herring.

Bryde's whales are solitary or appear in small groups of two or three. Their estimated worldwide population is 20,000 to 40,000.

7. Minke Whale

At 10 tons and 30 feet, minke whales are the smallest of the rorquals. These "slinky minkes" are hard to identify individually, and travel alone or in small groups. They can be identified by the white "wing patches" on their flippers and by their proportionately short narrow triangular rostrum or upper jaw.

Minkes are black on top, white below, and

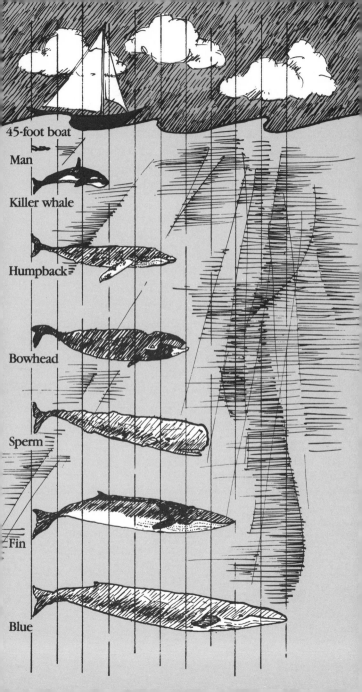

45-foot boat

Man

Killer whale

Humpback

Bowhead

Sperm

Fin

Blue

their baleen plates are yellowish-white. They lift their entire bodies out of the water when breaching, and then dive for up to 10 minutes. Minkes prefer the Arctic waters, and feed in the Northern Hemisphere on schooling fish such as cod and herring, or on krill.

Minkes can sometimes become fascinated with boats and people, will swim around boats, and may allow themselves to be touched. They tend to remain in inshore waters and (unusual for rorquals) will become stranded on occasion.

Because the larger rorquals have been so heavily fished, Japan, Norway and the USSR have over the past two decades increasingly concentrated their whaling on the minke, and this continues in the era of "scientific" research whaling. Current population estimate: 350,000+.

8. Right Whale

Traditionally, these whales were the "right" whales to hunt, since they swim slowly, inhabit coastal waters at breeding season, have lots of blubber and 7-foot-long baleen— and float when they have been killed. As a result, the right whale, also called the northern right whale, has become highly endangered. After a half century of protection from whaling, there are only 200-300 in the North Atlantic, a few hundred in the Northern Pacific, and 3,000-4,000 in the Southern Hemisphere. It is feared that the North Atlantic group may become so inbred (after depletion in its numbers) that it can no longer reproduce.

The right whale, a baleen whale, is a skimmer. This rotund whale (averaging 50-60 feet in length and 70 tons), swims slowly along the surface, its huge mouth agape, allowing large quantities of water to strain through its baleen, while plankton such as krill are trapped and swallowed.

Right whales are all black, with a white patch on the underside near the anus. They can be individually identified by the pattern of callosities (light-colored growths) on their heads.

Right whales compete for females, and courtship occurs year-round although breeding appears to be seasonal. Calves are 16-19 feet long at birth, and stay with the mother for about a year. In late 1987 in Patagonia, researchers from the Long Term Research Institute observed a mother nursing two calves for a period of several weeks, the first time this has been noted in a baleen female.

9. Bowhead Whale

Next to the right whale, the bowhead is probably the most threatened of the great whales. Researchers using acoustical underwater devices to listen to the bowhead's calls and songs have doubled previous estimates of Western Arctic bowhead population, and now believe that over 7,000-8,000 remain. A few hundred survive elsewhere in the Arctic. Alaskan Eskimos still engage in subsistence hunts for bowheads, and are at present allowed under International Whaling Commission quotas to strike 44 bowheads and land 41 each year.

The bowhead or Greenland right whale reaches a length of 60 feet and a weight of 65 tons, and is blue-black in color. An extremely slow-moving and stocky whale, it has a very large head and a mouth that is bowed upward (hence, possibly, its name). Its tongue weighs about one ton. The bowhead's 14-foot-long baleen is the largest of any whale. Like the Northern right whale, the bowhead skims the surface of the ocean, feeding on microplankton.

The bowhead follows the edge of the Arctic ice, protected from the cold by up to 4 feet of blubber. It is able to break through a foot of ice (it has no dorsal fin) in order to breathe, and can remain submerged for an hour. Belugas often accompany bowheads, perhaps to take advantage of the bowheads' superior ability to find breaks in the ice.

10. Gray Whale

Each year the gray whales of the Northern Pacific make an incredible migration from their summer feeding grounds in the Arctic seas along the coasts of Alaska, British Columbia, Washington, Oregon, and California to their winter calving grounds in the lagoons of Mexico's Baja California, and back again to the Arctic. This 10-14,000 mile round-trip is one of the longest mammal migrations, and a source of delight to coastal residents and boaters. (The State of California has designated the gray whale as its state marine mammal.)

Gray whales grow to a length of 45-50 feet and a weight of 30 tons. They are mottled gray in color, but whale lice and barnacles that attach themselves to the backs of gray whales give them scattered yellow and white patches. They have a narrow tapered head, knuckle-like bumps in lieu of a dorsal fin, yellow-white baleen plates, and thick furrows the length of their throats.

Gray whales are bottom feeders. They dive to the ocean floor, roll over and suck up the sediment at the bottom, retaining the small organisms, crustaceans and tube worms, and expelling the seawater, mud, and even kelp.

Gray whales can be identified by characteristic coloration and scars of the dorsal area, and fluke contours. Interested people can adopt individual gray whales through the Whale Center in Oakland, California, and receive a photograph and information about "their" gray whale.

Gray whales are not monogamous, and up to five males may vie for the favors of a single female. Mating is believed to take place on the southward migration, with birth over a year later in Baja. Calves are often seen riding on their mothers' backs.

Gray whales today are often friendly. Occasionally, some will approach small boats and allow themselves to be touched or petted. Ironically, they were labelled "devil fish" by early whalers because of their ferocity when they or their calves were harpooned.

The gray whale population is estimated to be 21,000. This is the only great whale that has regained its pre-commercial whaling numbers.

11. Killer Whale

*Exception might be taken to the name
bestowed upon this whale . . . For we are all
killers, on land and on sea; Bonapartes and
Sharks included.*

MELVILLE

A cetacean of the family *Delphinidae,* the
killer whale can be considered either a
medium-size whale or the largest of the
dolphins. Males can be 30 feet and 9 tons,
females 23 feet and 4 tons. They are perhaps
the fastest swimmers in the ocean.

Killer whales have 10 to 12 conical teeth
on each side of the upper and lower jaws,
and they use these interlocking teeth to good
advantage. They are carnivores, unlike other
whales, and feed on fish, squid, sea lions,
elephant seals, porpoises and small whales.
They have been seen to "play" with their
prey (in one case, a seal pup) for 20 minutes
before eating it. Killer whales hunt in packs,
and will even attack and kill blue whales.
Killer whales do not, however, attack
humans.

The dorsal fin is the killer whale's most
distinctive trait. Fins of mature males are
triangular and up to 6 feet high, while the

fins of females are 3 feet and falcate or curved. Killers have streamlined heads. They are black on top, except for a white patch behind each eye, and have clear black and white markings on their undersides.

Killer whales (which can be individually identified through coloration and dorsal fins) function in small "pods" or family groupings, which stay together for long periods of time, possibly for life. Killers make whistling and low frequency clicking sounds for identification and communication; some of these sounds are made only by members of a particular pod while others are shared with other pods. Sometimes pods will come together as a "super pod" featuring spyhopping, lobtailing, and speed swimming.

12. Beluga Whale

This medium-size toothed whale lives mainly in Arctic and sub-Arctic waters, and there is a small population in the St. Lawrence River. Its thick layer of blubber prevents heat from escaping. Beluga males average 15 feet in length and females about 13 feet. Having only a dorsal ridge, not a dorsal fin, it swims easily under floating ice. Unlike other whales, the beluga has unfused neck vertebrae and thus can turn its head. The beluga has a protruding forehead (called a "melon") which, as it changes shape, may play a role in echolocation. They have about 10 teeth in each side of both upper and lower jaws, but swallow their food whole.

Belugas, sometimes called "sea canaries" by sailors, emit high-pitched squeals, whistles, mewing, chirps, and clicks, and are among the most vocal of cetaceans.

Adult belugas are white in color, the reason that this species is also known as the "white" whale. Some also call it the "belukha" to avoid confusion with the beluga sturgeon of beluga caviar fame. Worldwide population estimate: 50-80,000.

13. Narwhal

There is no confusing this unicorn of the Arctic with other types of whales. The most prominent feature of mature male narwhals is the left tooth that grows through the front of the jaw to become a spiral ivory tusk 8-9 feet in length. It is believed that the tusk is used by battling males to assert dominance over other males in the competition to mate with females. Males also have a right tooth, but it rarely erupts through the gum; in females, a left tooth will erupt in rare instances. Since females are able to feed successfully without the tusk, it is not likely that the tusk is related to food-gathering.

Since no other single-tusked animal exists, the narwhal appears to be the basis of the unicorn legend. Narwhal tusks were used in the construction of the Pope's throne in Rome.

Like the bowhead whale and beluga, the narwhal spends its entire life in the Arctic, protected from cold by a 4-inch layer of blubber. It lacks a dorsal fin and can thus swim under the ice. Like all whales, the narwhal must breathe at regular intervals; thus the sudden closing of breathing holes in the ice is an ever-present danger.

Male narwhals reach about 15 feet in body length and weigh 3,500 pounds. Females are slightly smaller, but weigh only 2,000 pounds. Narwhals feed on squid, cod, flounder, shrimp, and crab.

The slow-swimming (about 4 m.p.h.) narwhals continue to be killed from the kayak in summer hunts by the Inuit of the Canadian Arctic and Western Greenland. The narwhal skin or mattaq (a source of Vitamin C) is eaten raw or boiled, and the meat is dried for consumption during the winter. The Inuit have a subsistence economy, and the hundreds of narwhals killed in an average year are extremely important to them. Current worldwide population of narwhals is estimated to be nearly 30,000.

14. Long-Finned Pilot Whale

A dolphin like the killer whale, the pilot whale is a darling of aquariums and zoos, is easily trained for water shows, and has even been taught to retrieve objects deep on the ocean floor.

Pilot whales run 16-20 feet in length and 2-3 tons. They exhibit a strongly curved dorsal fin, and have very long, sickle-shaped flippers. (The short-finned pilot whale is not quite so large and has much smaller flippers.) Pilot whales have a distinctive rounded head with a protruding forehead or melon, and for this reason they are also known as "pothead" whales. This whale appears to be totally jet black, and is sometimes called the "blackfish."

Pilot whales are very social, and can be seen in herds of several hundred. They also hunt in a group, forming a circle to trap their common prey. Pilot whales generally eat squid, with herring as second choice. They grasp the squid with the 8-10 large conical teeth they have on each side of their upper and lower jaws. Pilot whales also form feeding groups and resting groups. Unfortunately, these whales on occasion become stranded on beaches, sometimes in large numbers.

The present population of this whale is not known, but it is not considered an endangered species.

15. Dolphins and Porpoises

The dolphins, beings of the interface between air and water . . . are surely as close to magic at sea as we are likely to get.
RICHARD ELLIS, AUTHOR AND ARTIST

Most smaller cetaceans (under 12-15 feet) are classified as dolphins or porpoises. Dolphins have numerous conical teeth while porpoises have small, spade-shaped teeth. Unlike dolphins, porpoises do not have pointed beaks.

The bottlenose dolphin (which reachs 13 feet and 1,400 pounds) is the most familiar of all cetaceans. Well known through the *Flipper* TV program and movies of the 1970's, this dolphin is commonly kept in oceanariums, aquariums, and research facilities, where it delights with its swimming and leaping abilities (as do belugas, killer whales, and other dolphins and porpoises). Michelle Jeffries, head trainer at the Long Marine Lab, University of California, Santa Cruz, reports that dolphins are not only intelligent, but also manipulative, creative, and fun; they plot how to take control of a situation and how to amuse themselves.

Two other dolphins, the spotted and spinner dolphins, often swim directly above schools of yellowfin tuna. For this reason, they have been caught by the millions in the purse seine nets of tuna fishermen, and have died agonized deaths. A public outcry against this slaughter resulted in enactment of the 1972 Marine Mammal Protection Act. As a result, the "incidental kill" by the U.S. tuna fleet has been somewhat reduced through use of a smaller mesh net and a "back-down" procedure to release dolphins before the net is hauled aboard.

Slow progress by the U.S. fleet and backsliding by foreign fleets led to 1988 amendments to the MMPA. Henceforth, observers will be placed on all U.S. tuna vessels that set "on dolphin," sundown sets will be restricted, and foreign nations that fail to meet U.S. dolphin protection standards will face a total ban on the export of tuna to the U.S.

Other dolphins range from the 8-foot common dolphin, which may appear in herds of 2,000, to the 14-foot Risso's dolphin or Grampus.

The most common porpoise is the 4-6 foot, 150-pound harbor porpoise, which lives in the waters of the East and West coasts of the United States. It forms a graceful rolling arc as it breaks the surface of the ocean to breathe, and then returns.

Bonnet, Crossbeak, and Bone: Three Very Famous Whales

In early October, 1988, three young gray whales became trapped in frozen seas off Point Barrow, Alaska. Their plight was picked up by local and then national and international TV. Suddenly, the fate of Bonnet, Crossbeak, and Bone (also called Kanik or Snowflake by the local Inupiat Eskimos) became of intense interest worldwide.

Pleas for help reached President Reagan, who instructed the National Guard to do what it could. Eskimos cut breathing holes for the whales (who needed to surface every four minutes), industry responded, and two brothers-in-law came up from Minnesota with their company's bubbling de-icer that in fact kept the breathing holes from icing back up. Bone, sadly, became lost under the ice.

After three weeks, it was the Soviet icebreakers *Vladimir Arseniev* and *Admiral Makarov* that cleared a path to the open sea through which Bonnet and Crossbeak were coaxed.

Millions of dollars were spent to save what scientists agreed were three whales not needed for the continued recovery of the gray whale species. The impact on public opinion in the United States, Soviet Union, and other nations was, however, incalculable. *People Magazine* summed up the exercise this way: "If there was anything to lament in the colossal effort to save the whales, it was not that we care too much for another species, but that too often we care too little for our own."

There have been many other instances of humans saving whales in distress. Physty, a sperm whale (genus: *Physeter*), which beached on Coney Island, New York, was force fed squid and antibiotics and, after a week, was able to return to the open sea. Humphrey the humpback was induced to quit the Sacramento River and return to San Francisco Bay. U.S. naval personnel on duty in the Arabian Sea straddled a 40-foot female sperm whale and cut her out of the fishing net in which she was entangled. And in 1985 a Soviet icebreaker broke through ice up to 12 feet thick to rescue about 1,000 trapped belugas; however, it was only after the *Moskva* began to play classical music from its loudspeaker that the whales followed the ship to the open ocean.

Whalewatching

When you get next to a whale, you are completely awed by it. It reminds you . . . that you're not really the star of the show.
ROGER PAYNE

Whales and other cetaceans swimming and leaping in the open ocean are among the wonders of nature, and it is thus not surprising that whalewatching as a commercial/educational activity has boomed in the past decade. During months of whale activity (and decent weather), whale enthusiasts can choose from numerous whalewatching options all along the Pacific Coast, in the Gulf of Maine off New England, and elsewhere on the Atlantic seaboard. Some trips have resident naturalists on board.

When you're out whalewatching in a small ship or launch, you may see whales breaching or you may see porpoises, as described by author Joan McIntyre, "fooling around in the morning, splashing and leaping, gliding in twos and threes with long fluttering and beating lines, hugging and chasing and playing and talking to each other and to the sea."

In the wake of this increased whale-watching activity (also known as "non-consumptive utilization of cetacean resources") has come the need to regulate man's physical approach to the whales. For the Gulf of Maine, the U.S. National Marine Fisheries Service has issued voluntary "Whale Watch Guidelines" that advise boaters, when in sight of whales, to avoid excessive changes of speed or direction; to approach within 300 feet only at no wake or idle speed, and one

50

boat at a time; and not to approach intentionally within 100 feet. Regulations stricter than these guidelines are now in force for the humpback calving grounds off Maui in the Hawaiian Islands.

The trend may now be toward further legal restrictions on whalewatching. The November, 1988 Monterey conference on whalewatching recommended that the NMFS, after consultation with interested parties, issue enforceable regulations on a region-by-region basis.

Military Uses

We don't think it's ethical for human beings to use other intelligent beings to wage war . . . To impose a warrior's role on other forms of intelligent life that exist on our planet seems to go beyond the pale.

ROBBINS BARSTOW

One "new frontier" of human-cetacean interaction lies in the U.S. Navy's use of dolphins for underwater military missions. The Navy has confirmed that it uses trained dolphins to locate (but not to detonate) mines in the Persian Gulf. Details of the Navy's Marine Mammal Program have long been kept top-secret, but *Greenpeace* reports that dolphins "are being trained to detect, cripple and kill frogmen; aid in the retrieval of mines and assorted military hardware lost at sea; and attach listening devices or mines to enemy ships."

The Navy pledges not to use dolphins in situations where they could be killed or intentionally injured. However, dolphins have died during acclimatization, and corporal abuse has been reported. And it is unclear how they would defend themselves against frogmen they might be sent to attack.

One animal-rights activist, North Carolina State University professor Tom Regan, draws an interesting distinction between canine soldiers and dolphins. Dogs, Regan asserts, have made an implicit deal with humans in which we feed them and they in return assume certain obligations, but "by training dolphins for military purposes, we've entered their aquatic cave without being invited."

Adherents of using dolphins for military roles point to the likely saving of human life.

Save-The-Whales

Creation, and we as the responsible portion of it, are diminished by wanton behavior toward creatures that so stunningly exemplify the mysteriousness of the natural.

GEORGE WILL

In 1946, faced with the depletion of whales worldwide, 15 whaling nations formed the International Whaling Commission, designed, through regulation of the whaling industry, to safeguard for future generations "the great natural resources represented by the whale stocks." In its first decades, the IWC set very high quotas (up to 60,000 whales in some years) for the taking of different types of whales, so that one species after another became decimated.

Non-whaling nations, interested in the survival of whales, began to join the IWC. In 1982, the IWC voted a total moratorium on commercial taking of whales starting in 1986, with the moratorium to be reviewed in 1990. By 1988 all nations had agreed to the moratorium. (Under a non-commercial, "subsistence," whaling exception, the Soviet

Union is allowed to take 179 gray whales annually in the years 1989-91 for its aboriginal population, and Alaskan natives have been given a quota of 44 strikes and 41 landed bowheads per year.)

While official commercial whaling has ended for the time being, nations may engage in "scientific" whaling without IWC approval. Japan has proposed to kill 825 minke and 50 sperm whales per year, but limited its 1988 Antarctic catch to under 300 minkes. Japan also seeks to convince the IWC that its coastal whaling is similar to aboriginal whaling and should be exempt from the zero quota. Iceland, in a bilateral agreement with the U.S., agreed to limit its 1988 catch to 68 fins and 10 seis. Norway was to take up to 30 minkes during 1988.

Probably fewer than 1,000 whales were killed in 1988 in commercial (including "pirate" activity), "scientific," and aboriginal whaling. Clearly, great progress has been made in stopping the killing, especially of endangered species (although the aboriginal hunt of bowheads is of special concern).

The situation remains fluid, however. Whale meat is considered a delicacy in Japan, where it commands very high prices; it is thus no coincidence that Japan is at present the major whaling nation. Even the Icelandic whaling industry is based on sometimes secret export of whale meat to Japan. (Such a shipment was uncovered in Finland in 1988, and although not confiscated, was at least returned to Iceland.) Pressure for continuation of whaling in one form or another will continue.

Arrayed against the whaling industry in a political, economic, and public relations battle is the citizen-led save-the-whale movement, with the sometime support of the U.S. and other governments represented on the IWC.

Enforcement of U.S. laws is of central importance in this equation. The Endangered Species Act protects species that are "endangered" or "threatened;" blue, bowhead, fin, gray, humpback, right, sei and sperm whales have been so designated. These whales are thus automatically considered "depleted" under the Marine Mammal Protection Act. The Pelly Amendment to the Fishermen's Protective Act permits the president to embargo fish products, including processed fish, coral and cultured pearls, from nations (such as Japan and Norway) that "diminish the effectiveness of an international fisheries agreement" (like the

IWC zero quota for commercial whaling). The Packwood-Magnuson Amendment bars countries that violate an IWC ban from fishing in American territorial waters.

In 1988, more than a dozen environmental organizations sued the U.S. State and Commerce Departments for failure, in contravention of American law, to impose sanctions against Iceland for its "scientific" whaling. (It is thought that the U.S. need of continued access to its Icelandic airbase played a major role in this decision.) At the same time, threatened boycotts of fastfood chains such as Burger King and Wendy's have led them to cut back purchase of Icelandic fish, and some school districts have refused to buy Icelandic fish products.

In a few cases, marine sanctuaries (equivalent to underwater national parks) have been designated to protect whales. The Dominican Republic has designated Silver Bank sanctuary to protect humpbacks; Mexico in 1988 designated an enormous sanctuary in the Baja Peninsula to protect the calving grounds of the gray whale; and sanctuaries in the near future will be designated at Monterey Bay, California (gray, humpback and blue whales) and on the Outer Coast of Washington (killer whales) under the U.S. Marine Sanctuaries Program.

The Future of Whales

As we feel for ourselves, we must feel for all forms of life—the whales, the seals, the forests, the seas.

GREENPEACE PHILOSOPHY

Eight species of whales remain endangered. "Scientific" whaling of minke, fin, and sei whales continues. Subsistence whaling is permitted. The IWC moratorium on the harvesting of whales comes up for review in 1990. Japan has vowed that it will "never" end the killing of whales.

Only a committed, engaged citizenry, in the United States and in actual and potential whaling nations, together with concerned governments, can save many types of whales from continuing depredation and possible extermination.

"We have learned," says Dr. Roger Payne, "that all men are created equal, but the whales remind us that all *species* are created equal—that every organism on earth, whether large or small, has an inalienable right to life." We owe it to ourselves, not less than to the whales, to ensure that these noble creatures remain fruitful and multiply. Some day they may acknowledge our effort in a way that we can understand.

Appendix
Whale-Related Organizations

Non-Governmental

American Cetacean Society
P.O. Box 2639
San Pedro, CA 90731
(213) 548-6279
Protection of whales and dolphins internationally
through education of the public; publishes quarterly
"Whalewatcher"

Animal Protection Institute of America
PO Box 22505
Sacramento, CA 95822
(916) 731-5521
Education to save-the-whale; research

Animal Welfare Institute
P.O. Box 3650
Washington, DC 20007
(202) 337-2233
Education of the public to ensure whale survival

Center for Coastal Studies
59 Commercial Street
Provincetown, MA 02657
(508) 487-3622
Cetacean research; provides naturalists for
whale-watching

Center for Marine Conservation
1725 DeSales Street, NW
Washington, DC 20036

(202) 429-5609
Protection of marine wildlife through education
and policy-oriented research

Cetacean Society International
190 Stillwold Drive
Wethersfield, CT 06109
(203) 563-6444
International networking to save cetaceans on a
global basis; publications and newsletter

Defenders of Wildlife
1244 19th Street, NW
Washington, DC 20036
(202) 659-9510
Education to help save endangered species; active
on driftnet issue

Earth Island Institute
300 Broadway, Suite 28
San Francisco, CA 94133
(415) 788-3666
International marine mammal project; research,
education, publicity and direct action to save
dolphins in tuna fishing

Greenpeace USA
1436 U Street, NW
Washington, DC 20009
(202) 462-1177
Direct action; boycott of Icelandic fisheries products

Greenpeace (Canada)
578 Bloor Street West
Toronto, Ontario M6G 1K1
(416) 922-3011

Greenpeace (Australia)
Private Bag 6, Broadway P.O.
Sydney 2007 N.S.W.
(02) 2110089

Humane Society of the United States
2100 L Street, NW
Washington, DC 20037
(202) 452-1100
Political and consumer activists to save whales;
boycotts of Japanese, Icelandic fish

International Wildlife Coalition
320 Gifford Street
Falmouth, MA 02540
(508) 540-8086
Promotion of end to whaling through education,
advocacy, boycotts; Adopt-A-Whale (humpbacks)

Long Term Research Institute
191 Weston Road
Lincoln, MA 01773
(617) 259-0423
Research, education and conservation; affiliate of
World Wildlife Fund

Sea Shepherd Conservation Society
P.O. Box 7000-S
Redondo Beach, CA 90277
(213) 373-6979
International and local direct action and confrontation;
scuttling of whaling vessels

Whale and Dolphin Conservation Society
22 Hughenden Road
Weston-super-Mare
Avon BS23 2UR
United Kingdom
(0934) 621089
Education of public as to cetacean problems worldwide

Whale Center
3929 Piedmont Avenue
Oakland, CA 94611
(415) 654-6621
Whale conservation, lobbying on national and
international levels; Whalebus; gray whalewatching;
adopt-a-(gray)whale

Wildlife Conservation International
New York Zoological Society
Bronx, NY 10460
(212) 220-5197
Research project in Hawaii on humpback whales

Governmental

International Whaling Commission
The Red House
Station Road, Histon
Cambridge CB4 4NP
United Kingdom
(0220) 233971
Sets quotas on commercial and subsistence whaling;
reviews "scientific" research whaling

U.S. Marine Mammal Commission
1625 I Street
Washington, DC 20006
(202) 653-6237
Monitors Federal actions, makes recommendations
on marine mammal protection

National Marine Fisheries Service
National Oceanic and Atmospheric Administration
U.S. Department of Commerce
1335 East-West Highway
Silver Spring, MD 20910
(301) 427-2276
Enforces Marine Mammal Protection Act; develops
international negotiating positions; Administrator is U.S.
delegate to IWC

Selected Resources

Minasian, S.M., Balcomb and Foster, *The World's Whales: The Complete Illustrated Guide* (Smithsonian Books, 1984)

Barstow, Robbins, *Meet The Great Ones* (Cetacean Society International, 1987)

Slijper, E., *Whales and Dolphins* (University of Michigan Press, 1976)

Ellis, Richard, *The Book of Whales* (Alfred A. Knopf, Inc., 1980)

McIntyre, Joan, *The Delicate Art of Whale Watching* (Sierra Club Books, 1982)

"Whale Fact Pack," "Whalewatcher," and "Whale News" (American Cetacean Society)